LAURA K. MURRAY

FAIRIES

ARE THEY REAL?

CREATIVE EDUCATION · CREATIVE PAPERBACKS

Published by Creative Education and Creative Paperbacks
P.O. Box 227, Mankato, Minnesota 56002
Creative Education and Creative Paperbacks are imprints of The Creative Company
www.thecreativecompany.us

Design and production by **Christine Vanderbeek**
Art direction by **Rita Marshall**
Printed in the United States of America

Photographs by Alamy (Moviestore collection Ltd), Corbis (Bettmann, Blue Lantern Studio, Fine Art Photographic Library, Guy Heitmann/Design Pics), Dreamstime (Sjhuls), Getty Images (Science & Society Picture Library, Jan Stromme), iStockphoto (FairytaleDesign, Maximastudio), Mary Evans Picture Library (120 Great Fairy Paintings/Dover Publications Inc., Children's Book Illustrations/Dover Publications Inc., Imps, Elves, Fairies, & Goblins/Dover Publications Inc., Peter & Dawn Cope Collection), Shutterstock (Marcin Sylwia Ciesielski, Dragan85, Matt Gibson, Jenn Huls, Atelier Sommerland)
Illustration on p. 21 © 1983 by Monique Felix

Library of Congress Cataloging-in-Publication Data
Murray, Laura K.   Fairies / Laura K. Murray.   p. cm. – (Are they real?)   Includes index.   Summary: A high-interest inquiry into the possible existence of magical fairies, emphasizing reported sightings and stories as well as investigations into fairy rings.

ISBN 978-1-60818-763-8 (hardcover)   **ISBN 978-1-62832-371-9** (pbk)   **ISBN 978-1-56660-805-3** (ebook)
This title has been submitted for CIP processing under LCCN 2016008268.

CCSS: RI.1.1, 2, 4, 5, 6, 7, 10; RI.2.1, 2, 4, 5, 6, 7; RI.3.1, 2, 5, 6, 7; RF.1.1, 2, 3, 4; RF.2.3, 4; RF.3.3, 4

First Edition HC 9 8 7 6 5 4 3 2 1   **First Edition PBK** 9 8 7 6 5 4 3 2 1

CONTENTS

A TINY DANCE

A man walks down a country road at night. He hears music. He sees a circle of light on the ground.

INSIDE THE CIRCLE ARE TINY, DANCING PEOPLE!

TRICKY SPRITES

People think fairies are magical **SPRITES**. Most love to play tricks on humans. They may live in houses, forests, or water. They may live underground, in hills, or in **FAIRY RINGS**. Are fairies real or make-believe?

WHAT DO FAIRIES LOOK LIKE?

Fairies can be beautiful or ugly. They can be good or bad, too.

They may look like small humans with wings.

Some can even change shape. They stay hidden.

WHAT DO FAIRIES DO?

Fairies invite humans to play and dance. But fairies get upset easily!

They use magic to make things look beautiful. Mean fairies are said to steal human babies.

Some **SCIENTISTS** study fairy rings in fields, lawns, and forests. They say the rings come from things growing underground.

STORIES OF FAIRIES

In 1917, Elsie Wright and Frances Griffiths took photos of fairies in England.

FRANCES GRIFFITHS

A 1997 MOVIE CALLED FAIRYTALE WAS MADE ABOUT FRANCES AND ELSIE.

Were the fairies real? Many people thought so. Years later, the girls said most of the pictures were fake.

Fairies appear in many famous stories.
Cinderella has a kind fairy godmother.

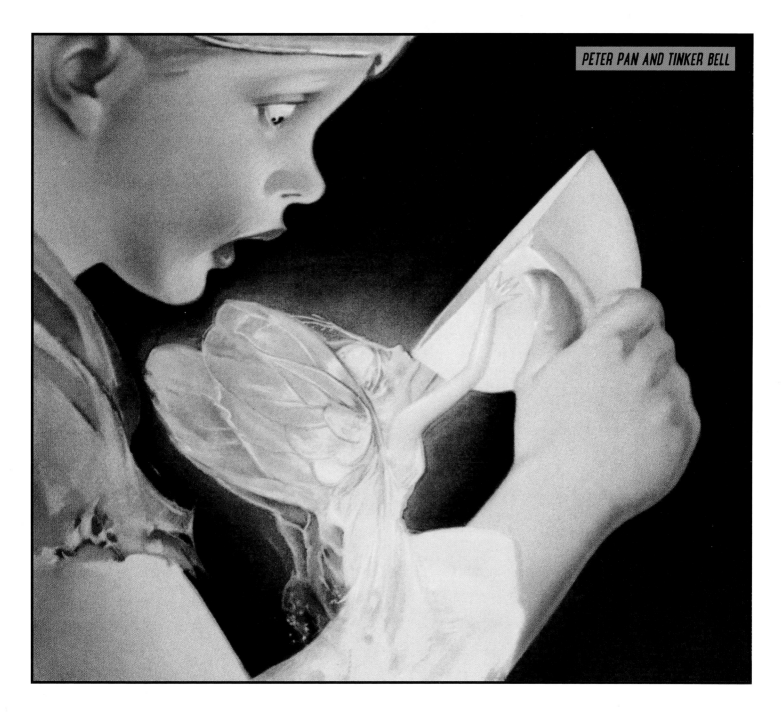

Peter Pan has his friend Tinker Bell. William
Shakespeare often wrote about fairies in his plays.

17

FAIRY ENCOUNTERS

People believed in fairies long ago. They used fairies to explain the unknown. Most people today say fairies are just **FOLKLORE**. But could there be a fairy world we cannot see?

What would you do if
you saw a fairy?

REMEMBER, YOU CANNOT ALWAYS TRUST A FAIRY!

INVESTIGATE IT!
MAKE A FAIRY GARDEN

Find a small box or container. Add dirt, flowers, plants, rocks, or shells. Place a container of water in the box. This will be a fairy pond. You can make a small bench or table, too. Do you think fairies will visit?

GLOSSARY

FAIRY RINGS circles of mushrooms said to be magical

FOLKLORE popular stories or beliefs that are passed on through the years

SCIENTISTS people who study how the world works

SPRITES fairies or elves

READ MORE

Porter, Steve. *Fairies*. Minneapolis: Bellwether Media, 2014.

Savery, Annabel. *Fairies*. Mankato, Minn.: Smart Apple Media, 2013.

WEBSITES

Fairy Coloring Page

http://www.coloring.ws/fairies1.htm

Choose a fairy picture to print and color.

Fairy Tales, Folktales, and Classic Stories

http://www.dltk-teach.com/rhymes/

Find activities and crafts about famous fairy tales.

Note: Every effort has been made to ensure that the websites listed above are suitable for children, that they have educational value, and that they contain no inappropriate material. However, because of the nature of the Internet, it is impossible to guarantee that these sites will remain active indefinitely or that their contents will not be altered.

INDEX